YOUR GUIDE IN YOUTH SPORTS

JOHN A. DEANGELO

The contents of this work, including, but not limited to, the accuracy of events, people, and places depicted; opinions expressed; permission to use previously published materials included; and any advice given or actions advocated are solely the responsibility of the author, who assumes all liability for said work and indemnifies the publisher against any claims stemming from publication of the work.

All Rights Reserved
Copyright © 2019 by John A. DeAngelo

No part of this book may be reproduced or transmitted, downloaded, distributed, reverse engineered, or stored in or introduced into any information storage and retrieval system, in any form or by any means, including photocopying and recording, whether electronic or mechanical, now known or hereinafter invented without permission in writing from the publisher.

Dorrance Publishing Co
585 Alpha Drive
Suite 103
Pittsburgh, PA 15238
Visit our website at *www.dorrancebookstore.com*

ISBN: 978-1-6442-6965-7
eISBN: 978-1-6442-6317-4

INTRODUCTION

So you just became proud parents of your first child. There will be so many great moments, as well as some scary ones: the baby's first steps, first words, first illness, and so on. You started the baby album from the very beginning in what you hope will bring joy to everyone in the family with wonderful memories. You plan on looking at this album sometime after your child gets married and you're old and gray. Before we get that far, there are so many things that will happen before then. Everyone wants to see the baby, and you, as proud parents, are thrilled to show all. Before you know it, the baby turns one — how quick the first year went. They start getting toys and figures to play with, and soon after that they get a bat and a baseball. You roll the ball at them and watch all the different expressions each time. You watch as they play with all the toy figures, cars, trains, dolls, and more as the year goes by. Soon they are off to nursery school, Pre-K, and, before you know it, kindergarten. Now they are interacting with other children on a regular basis; they will come to like some things and dislike others. This book will help you introduce your child to the world of sports. We will cover from grammar school all the way through the high school years. We will talk about every age bracket in detail and the different organizations out there to help you decide which one fits your child the best. We will discuss different situations that might take place and the advantages and disadvantages of sports. We'll talk about school and sports and how to balance it. This book, at some point, will focus on you as a parent and as a possible coach. It will tell you what to look for in a coach and what to do if you feel the coach is out of line in handling your child. I hope by the time you're done reading this book, it will prepare you for what to look for if your child decides sports is for them. I hope this is a helpful guide from the very beginning because you're looking at ten to twelve years of sports ahead of you.

SPORTS START AT HOME

I am a firm believer that you don't sign up your child with any local organization until they enter first grade. Today we have parents signing up their children as young as three years old with sports organizations. Almost all organizations take kids by the time they turn four or five years old. This might be for only one or two hours a week, but they are signed up. This is a mistake for a few reasons. One, the child attention span at that age is short. They want to play for a short while, but then they start playing among themselves or just start doing things like running around on their own. It's like a new toy they beg you to get, then after a while it's on to something else. If your child is in a group of twenty kids with one instructor, no way is he or she controlling that group. Even if you have two instructors, it's still hard even if you split the two groups. The second reason I'm against it is because you will burn them out. Now the organization won't tell you this because they want your money. It's sad to say, but some organizations are not just happy with getting by from year to year. They run the organization like a business. If you think I'm kidding, we will touch on this later in the book. So now what do you do to keep them occupied and interested? It's your child — you and family members should be introducing the child to every sport. This not only is a great bonding experience, but you get to see what the child likes and what they don't like. Let the aunts, uncles, grandmothers, and grandfathers introduce them to different things. Who takes them to the park to go on the swings or play in the sandbox? Who has a catch with them? Someone else plays with them with their building blocks. Notice of all things I listed, I only listed one thing that is an actual sport. That's because you want them to try everything, enjoy everything, and introduce them to everything. Now you can see another reason why you don't need to sign up with an organization until first grade. By the time they are ready for first grade, you know what sport to start with, and you saved money by doing it this way. This is money that now can go toward your child's education instead of a sports organization. If you're thinking you did not save much, well if you started the child at four years old, you saved at least five hundred dollars by doing it my way, and that's only one child. You're not only saving money, but your child is bonding with family members and learning about family values. This is important to instill in a child at a young age because as they get older and make more friends, they spend less time with family. You hope that you did a good job with them that they remember to keep family near and dear to them throughout their lives. I remember great times with family when I was a child, and as I got older, I saw them less, but I made it a point to keep in touch with them no matter what with a phone call, a visit, or an email. When I was a child, we had all the things I talk about except this next item. I just heard from a coworker who says she got her twenty-one-month-old an iPad. I am young at heart but old school, so let's just say I'm glad I was a kid when I was a kid. We watched cartoons and education shows and learned from that, as well as from the family. It's bad enough today, whether I'm on the bus or in the street, it seems like everyone has a device in their hands. They don't read the newspapers; they read the newspapers off their phones. So your child will do the very same thing one day but let them grow up first. Let school introduce them to all the different technologies. Right now let them be a child. I'm all for children learning, and that's a good thing, and it's important. It's a good thing when the child starts counting and saying words, but that should come from family members and nursery school, not from some device at such a young age. We have enough grown-ups who are zombies with this technology stuff; let your children be children, and then when they get older, they can become zombies. I myself am at fault with my cell phone. Do you know that once I got my cell phone and entered all my numbers, I no longer remember everyone's number? That's because it's in my phone — no need to use my brain anymore, the phone has every number I need. So yes, I am a zombie too when it comes to my phone. Let's not do that to young children. Let them experience childhood first.

SOME THOUGHTS ON EACH SPORT

This is just to give you an idea of how long each season goes and how time-consuming it is. Since most seasons start in the fall when school starts, we will start with those sports.

Flag football starts in September and ends in December. This is the alternative to tackle football. I would definitely start with flag football before trying tackle football. In fact, with all we know today, I would not start a child in tackle until he is twelve years old. Flag football is also less expensive than tackle football.

With flag you will most likely play once or twice on the weekends with a practice during the week.

Basketball is another option. A regular in-house season can go from November to March or, in some cases, January to March. It depends on the organization you play with. Practices are minimal because it's in-house. If it were travel, it would be much more time-consuming.

If you're just starting out, start with in-house, then go to travel.

Baseball is the longest of all seasons. In-house can run from January indoors to June with the season starting in April. They practice indoors to see how the kids do to place them on teams.

If you're going to play travel, brace yourself and get used to having no life. Travel teams now play from April to September or October and practice year-round.

Again I suggest in-house, and then if you think your child is ready and committed, go to travel baseball.

Soccer is another option. They play indoor and outdoor. Indoor runs roughly from December to March while outdoor runs from March to May, but it varies at different organizations.

I prefer outdoor as opposed to indoor because outdoor is the real thing. The kids learn more.

Ice hockey is the toughest of sports because getting ice time is rough. You will do a lot of travelling in some cases just to get to a rink to practice. Ice hockey is another expensive sport, especially if your child is the goaltender. They wear the most equipment, and it's expensive.

Some places have field hockey. You might want to start with that; it's more local and less travelling.

Lacrosse is a great sport if you son or daughter is interested. It has become big over the years, and as long as your child is athletic, he or she can go out for the high school team with little or no experience. I've seen it happen.

Some other options, mostly for girls, would be volleyball, which has a fall and spring season, as well as dance.

However, dancing involves a lot of practice and travelling to competitions. I say go for it if your daughter is interested and committed.

Today golf is big with young children. Many areas have a golf course that teaches children from an early age. If they like it, why not? Everyone has a special talent; the key is finding it.

I didn't pick up a golf club until I was thirty-nine, but I understand today is different, and golf is certainly an option if your child likes it.

Remember, it's not about you; it's about your child. I believe all kids should be involved in something. It does not have to be a sport. It could be music. Maybe they are good at playing a certain instrument. Just as long as they stay active with something outside of school.

SCHOOL WORK COMES FIRST ALL THE TIME

So your child wants to play organized sports. This is great, but before you start, you make one thing clear. If he or she is going to play on a team, schoolwork must be completed before leaving for a practice or game. If it's a weeknight, unless the next day is an off day, this should be mandatory. If it's on weekends, you can be flexible, but it must get done. If not, then it's off the team.

At no time do you let them get away with not following this rule because then it could become a habit, and it's a habit that is not good. If your child someday makes it big in sports, that's great, but if he doesn't, you want him to be able to fall back on his education. You stress education comes first, and if she does well in school, she is free to play whatever sport she wants, assuming you're fine with that sport and her grades stay up. I say assuming you're fine with a certain sport because this writer was forbidden to play tackle football no matter how hard I tried.

When I was young, I did not understand this, but I have to say, as I got older, I understood why my parents did not want me to play football. Especially today with all the new technology we have, we see how taking so many hits affects the body and mind in the years to come. You hear former players who are crippled today tell their stories, one worse than the next. It does not change the fact that I enjoy the game, but I certainly understand why my parents did not want me to play football. We will never know the answer, but they might have saved my life.

So once your children understand schoolwork comes first, now you have to also make them understand they are committed to the team. Just like their homework has to be done, they are now part of a team, and they have a responsibility to be at every practice and every game unless they are sick or have an important family matter.

Under no circumstances can they skip practice or a game to go hang out with friends. Make them understand that this is a commitment, and if you are making time so they can play, then they have to be fully committed.

If they should get lazy with their work, you remind them that they will have to quit the team. If they don't want to play anymore, that's fine — never push a child — but if it's just being lazy, then you remind them that they are letting their teammates down. You remind them what it means when you make a commitment. You remind them they have to be dedicated. You also remind them that you are making sacrifices to get them to and from practices and games. You do it because you want to see them happy and enjoy their childhood, but if they are going to slack off, maybe it is time to quit the team.

We don't want this to be the case because then they will get the idea they can quit anything, so before you make it final, you make sure you sit down and discuss everything with them.

You need to cover all the pros and cons. From your viewpoint, you want them to stay with it so they have an interest in something and get to interact with other children and make new friends.

You do not want your child to be isolated. He needs to be involved in some kind of after-school activity. So before he says he's had enough of something, make sure he has something else to move on to. Make sure you covered what he will be missing and why quitting is not a good idea. Then if he absolutely wants to stop, you move on to something until you find what activity fits him best.

IT'S TIME TO JOIN A SPORTS ORGANIZATION

Your child is entering first grade. Her friends are playing sports, and she wants to play too. If you choose to let her join before grade school, then if your experience was a good one, you would most likely stay with that organization.

If this is your first experience at this, then you should look at it this way. You want to play with the organization closet to your home if possible. This cuts down on travel, and if you're both working, it makes it easier that your commute to and from is short as well.

If your child is in a Catholic school, and it has a sports program, I firmly believe your child should play for that organization if you and the child are comfortable with it. Your child gets to represent the school he attends. That is a wonderful feeling; it gives him a sense of pride and a sense of closeness to the school.

If you're sending your child to a public school, you want to join an organization close to home, the reason being, once again, it cuts down on travel for all individuals involved. If it's a private school, sometimes it has a good after-school sports programs and you can stay there for everything. If it doesn't, then it goes back to trying to stay close to home.

No matter what your scenario is, make sure you research the organization before you sign up your child. Ask people you know who have kids playing there already. If it's the organization where your child goes to school, ask within the school. Go on the organization website — by now everyone has a website. Research the history of the organization. Don't be afraid to introduce yourself to one of the directors and see if it's the place for your child to play. Once you settle on an organization, learn as much as you can and watch how they handle the kids. Most likely all will go well, but as you will see later on, sometimes issues arise. Learn as much as you can about the coaches, their history, background, etc. These are the men and women who will be in charge of your kids; you want to know as much as possible.

Another thing to look at is the cost to play. We know everything is expensive today, but some organizations out there are money hungry and charge much more than others. Remember, this is the grammar school level. Your child is most likely being coached by a volunteer, not a paid professional. Feel free to ask the person when you sign up your child how the organization came to that price. If the breakdown seems fair to you, fine, but if not, don't hesitate to ask questions. No doubt the organization has expenses but ask them to break it down. If you're signing your child up for soccer, the cost should only be related to soccer. In that fee should not be twenty-five dollars for baseball. During the year, they will do various fundraisers where you will be asked to buy tickets. This is the norm with all organizations. It's understandable and acceptable; what's not acceptable is you supporting a sport your child does not participate in.

If an organization does its math right, each sport should support itself. If the sport your child is playing needs a fundraiser to help it, you support it, as long as that money goes to the sport your child is playing. Today too many organizations are money hungry; the more they get, the more they want. In a time when everything is going up, you want to find an organization that understands that and just wants to meet the needs to support the sport your child is playing in.

Some sports are more than others; that is understandable. For example baseball is very expensive as opposed to basketball. Always get a breakdown at the start. It's your money. You have a right to know what you're paying for.

COACHING YOUR CHILD

Coaching your child can be fun, it can be interesting, and it can be a nightmare. I am not in favor of parents coaching their child, but in this day and age, it happens often. Let's take a look at the different possibilities.

The only way it can be fun is if the parent understands that she must treat her child like all the other kids on the team. Then it's possible it can work out. If the parent favors her child, then there is no question she will hear it from the parents of the other players.

It can be interesting because it's no longer parent, it's coach. The child is following instructions at home, and now he is on a team and has to follow instructions not from his dad but from his coach. The child might think the dad is being unfair at times; the coach might be harder on his kid than he is on the others. Or he might go easy on his son while working everyone else harder.

It can be a nightmare because now it's never over. Whatever happens in practice or a game gets talked about at home. You're with your coach at practice or a game, and then you're with your mom at home. This can be hard on both, as well as all the members of the family.

I am against it because I think it's good for kids to learn how to deal with other individuals starting from a young age. If a child had a stranger as a coach as opposed to a parent, she would be focused more. She knows she can't get away with anything; she is just like all the others on the team.

If your child is playing in-house, it's good that they get different coaches each year so that they learn from different coaches. This is like having different teachers in the classroom. If you're playing travel ball, chances are you will be with the same coach for a few years. This, in a way, is good because all parties will know what to expect from each other by the time the second year starts. Remember, travel ball in any sport is different. It's very competitive, and it's to everyone's advantage to stay with the same coach. It helps team chemistry if it's done right.

If you have to coach your child, treat he or she the same as everyone else. Don't make them the *coach's kid*. By that I mean, place your child where he or she fits best on the team.

If the sport is baseball, and he belongs in right field and bat seventh, don't put him up first and playing shortstop. This is a bad move for everyone.

If the sport is basketball, don't give her more playing time than all the other kids. Give her what she deserves. If you do this, you avoid what we call coach's kid syndrome. Make your daughter the same as everyone else on the team — no special or unfair treatment. Treat everyone the same, and you will have a great season, win or lose.

STAYING WITH THE SPORT YOUR CHILD LOVES TO PLAY

Once your child gets to be ten or eleven and he or she is overall a good athlete but really excels in one sport, maybe it's time to focus on just that one sport. There are numerous factors to consider here. The first thing is who came to the decision. If the child comes to the parent, it's something to really consider because he is telling you he doesn't want to play any other sport than this particular one. This means he really enjoys it, and he realizes that if he has a chance to play high school sports, it will be in this sport. The first thing you as a parent should do is sit down and discuss it with the child. Find out why he came to this decision and then give him the pros and the cons. The very first thing you tell him is he can do that as long as his grades stay up. If the grades fall, then it's off the team because school comes first. The second thing you make very clear to him is all the time and energy he has to put into the sport. He has to make a total commitment, and at the end of the day, he might not make it on his high school team. Give him numbers and show him how many kids play and how many only get to a certain level and never make it to the college or professional level. You're not trying to discourage him, but you're being honest with him. You make it clear to him that he might be the one enjoying what he is doing while keeping his grades up, but it's Mommy and Daddy who are devoting their time driving him around. For example if the sport happens to be hockey, that is not only time-consuming but also expensive. You explain everything to him. By now he is old enough to understand. Parents of a child playing hockey have to be up early in the morning, depending on how far they have to travel to get to the rink. Ice time is either given very early in the morning or late at night. The games are played throughout the state or in different states. I use hockey as a prime example, but no matter what the sport is, it will require the same dedication and commitment. Your child will be playing the sport year-round with very little free time to do anything else. If her friends are going somewhere, and she has a game or a practice, she should be going to the team event first. If she can join her friends later, fine, but true dedication means just that. There are very few exceptions, and you as parents want to be supportive but firm. Remember, your child made the choice, and there are times you will have to remind her of that and the sacrifices that come with it. Remind her of the sacrifices you made by missing your own gatherings with friends or relatives because she had to be somewhere for a game or a practice with you. If at some point the child wants to stop and be a regular kid again, sit her down just to reassure her that's what she wants and be supportive with her decision. She tried it and kept her grades up, but now she decided it's not for her. Don't scold them for wasting your time. Be supportive and understanding. Be thankful because now you get part of your life back too.

Now let's look at it from the other side. Let's say it's the parent who encourages the child to pick one sport because he is good at this one particular sport. The parent thinks this is the sport the child will be able to excel in at the high school level and maybe even in college.

This is a big mistake on the parent's part for a few reasons. You're forcing your child to do something he might not want to do. By doing this, the child might accept it, or he might reject the idea. He might even go along with it until he can't stand it anymore just to try and make you happy. All four scenarios are bad for everyone involved. By doing so, is the parent trying to live his or her life through the child? It's possible he was this close to making a professional ball club and was the last cut. Now he is trying to relive his dream through his child, which is a big mistake. I grew up with a kid in that exact situation, and it did not end well. When the kid played, he was miserable, but he did it for his dad. So the kid accepted it but did not enjoy it — not good for the kid at all.

YOUR GUIDE IN YOUTH SPORTS

If the kid rejects your idea, accept it and move on. Let her be a kid and enjoy her, especially if her grades are good. She will find something she is good at; it has to be her choice at a young age. If this was high school and she was graduating and going to college and was having trouble picking a major, of course you could try and guide her. That is totally different; it's a life decision. Youth sports is supposed to be fun for all, so enjoy it. Don't let it be a job for you or her. If you force the issue, she might turn on you. The grades might suffer, and you don't want that.

So if the kid picks one sport and continues to do well in school, just be supportive and watch him or her grow.

BE A SPECTATOR, NOT AN AGITATOR

So your child is signed up with an organization you feel comfortable with. You did your research, you checked the history of the organization, and you're happy with what you learned. That means it's now time for your child to play ball, but it's also time for you to just sit back and watch. Cheer your child on. Encourage them. Don't put them down because of something that took place on the field. They are learning and having fun; that is what it's all about. It's not about perfection. Don't push them to the point where they get turned off and don't want to play anymore. Don't tell them, "Well you should have made that play," or, "You need to do it this way."

You can practice with him on the side in your spare time but only if he wants to. Don't force him. Don't tell him he has to practice. Let him be a kid; let him do other things. Maybe he wants to go to the movies with friends or watch television instead of getting in extra practice with you. Forcing him will only turn him off, and you don't want that. Every child needs balance.

Don't make her feel guilty either. Don't start saying things like, "When I was younger, I played every chance I got." Your child is your child, but she is not you. As long as she attends practice, shows up for games, and plays her best, win or lose, that's all you should be concerned about from that standpoint.

Now if you feel the coach is shortchanging your child as far as playing time, you can question it, but whatever the answer is, you have to accept it. Then once the season is over, you decide to stay or leave the organization.

If the coach is abusive toward your child, now we have a bigger issue. You must first report it to the league director or president. Do not confront the coach; you can pull your child, but don't get into an argument with the coach. You speak to the director or president of the organization. Let the league officials handle it and get back to you. Maybe they will get you and the coach together to try and solve it. If you're not happy, then depending on how big of an issue it is, you decide if you want to pursue it legally.

This is something I hate to see in youth sports today, but the fact is it exists, and it exists way too much in this day and age. In my opinion, this happens because coaches forget it's not about winning but about the children. These kids are here to learn and have fun, but some coaches take it way to seriously, and as a result, this is what happens.

At this stage, it's about learning, having fun, and making friends. Later on when we describe the different levels of play, we will discuss which levels are tougher than others. Right now at the start, when children are anywhere from six to eight, it's all about them. Winning should be secondary, and today most coaches can't separate the two. This is why we hear stories of coaches and parents fighting at the baseball fields. Or parents fighting in the stands at a football or basketball game. You should cheer on your child's team and let the coaches coach and the officials officiate.

YOUR CHILD'S HEALTH IS IMPORTANT

Every parent wants a healthy baby, but sometimes that does not happen. Depending on what the medical issue is, if your doctor says he can play sports, then you get him involved. The doctor might give you restrictions, and you follow them for the best interest of your child. Maybe the child can play some sports but not others; it's all up to what the doctor says.

When you sign up your child, you make sure the organization knows of the child's condition. Once it assigns your child to a team, you make sure you introduce yourself to the coach and inform him or her of your child's condition and any instructions that go with it. You might have informed the organization when you signed your child up, but you want to make sure that message was passed on to the coach. These coaches are volunteers, so if you feel they can't handle it, then it's up to you to ask that your child be moved to another team. Whatever you do, you do not hide the condition by not saying anything to anyone. One, you're putting your child's health in jeopardy, and two, you're not being fair to the organization by not informing them of your child's condition.

I can't tell you how many kids I worked with in forty years that I was able to spot some form of illness in the child. Just from the way the child moved or talked I could tell something was not right. In some cases, the parent told the organization, and it was told to me as well, but in some cases, no one said anything. If I felt it was important, I went and spoke to the parents. If it was almost nonexistent, I left it alone and dealt with it, but in most cases, I did approach the parents. If this was the case, I spoke to them in a professional manner and made sure that they knew their child would be treated like all the others as far as playing time, but I would give them as much attention as I could. The parents appreciated that very much. They were thankful, and, as for me, it gave me a chance to help a child and make a difference.

If this same child was given to another coach, the results might have been different. Maybe the coach could not deal with it; maybe he wanted to focus on winning, and this child held him back. This attitude would be totally unacceptable, but there are many coaches out there who forget why they are there. An attitude like that might discourage the child, and you as a parent have every right to let your feelings be known to the league president. Hopefully both of you can get the situation corrected or place the child with someone who understands the situation better.

Some organizations have it on the registration form, and they ask you of any conditions your child has that they should be aware of. 1 have always been in favor of having this on the form, but believe it or not, some organizations do not ask. This is a huge mistake for everyone. You're putting your child in someone else's hands; it does not matter if it's for one hour a week or ten hours, everyone has the right to know. Don't hide it from anyone. You will only be hurting your child.

WHAT TO LOOK FOR IN COACHES

If you look up the word coach, you will see various words, but all connect to each other. It says a coach is a teacher, trainer, mentor, and instructor, all of which are true. Nowhere does it talk about the qualities a coach should have, especially someone who is coaching children.

The first thing a coach of young children should have is patience. If you are going to coach and you have a short fuse, coaching is not for you. A coach needs to be understanding, as well as caring. If you're coaching a clinic or at the instructional level, it's all about learning while having fun.

Once the children start playing games, you need those same qualities in a coach. If the coach starts focusing on winning and shortchanging kids of playing time, this coach does not belong coaching young children.

You also should watch the coach as he coaches the game. Does he get angry toward the children or the opponent or officials? Does he use vulgar language? If he is good during practices but turns into a different coach while coaching games, you either pull your kid off the team or go talk to the person in charge of the organization. If you do that and you're not satisfied, then move to another organization.

I have seen coaches who forget why they are there. They put winning ahead of the child's development and learning experience. You want the child to come back the following year. If the child has a bad experience with the coach, chances are she do not want to play for that coach the following year.

A good coach is one who can motivate, one who can get each child to reach his or her full potential while making sure each is having fun. Winning at the grammar school level is secondary, but lessons learned during this time can be used later on in life.

For example, is the coach being a good sportsman? Is he teaching his players good sportsmanship? If the coach is expressing poor sportsmanship, chances are the children will follow, and you don't want this for your child. This reminds me of a story of a young boy who played for the same coach for four years, age ten through thirteen. This boy was a good shooter, the best shooter on the team. The boy knew it, and he knew his coach needed him and he would never get in trouble, no matter what he did. As the years went on, the boy got better, but his attitude got worse because his coach never kept him in line. So now the eighth grade season is over, and high school is the next step for this child. He should be a lock to make his high school team, and he himself knew he had a good shot as well.

So his freshman year began in September at his new school, and the boy could not wait for tryouts in October. The day for tryouts finally arrived, and he was all excited. Tryouts run for a few days so coaches can give the kids a chance to see what they can do before they make their cuts. On the very first day, the coach instructed the group to do push-ups and wanted them to get as low as possible to the floor. So the boy, doing what he always did, made a wisecrack to the coach. The coach walked over to him and told him to leave the gym and don't come back. The boy, who was likely the best shooter in the gym, was cut on the first day of tryouts because of his attitude. This traces back to his grammar school coach who let him get away with everything. Had this boy had a coach to teach him right from wrong instead of just worrying how many points the boy scored, the boy would have had a nice high school career, as well as a good experience. Instead he never made it past the first day of tryouts because he had a grammar school coach who never took the time to teach him the core values of sports.

You also want a coach who is committed to coaching, not one who shows up when he wants to and hands the team off to others when he feels like it. If you're getting your child to every practice, every game, then the coach should be making the same effort. It's important the kids see the same coach. He is their leader, and he must lead by example. If the kids see a coach who comes and goes when he feels like it, they will do the same. As a parent, if this is happening, you have a right to speak to the director.

PERSONALITIES

Now you might be saying, why do we need to talk about personalities? What does that have to do with my child learning how to play sports? I'm not only going to talk about your child, but I'll talk about the team, as well as the coach. We will look at it from three different angles. First let's look at your child. Your child might be shy while her teammate might be a talker. Maybe we have a child who cries on the team. Then there might be someone who is very aggressive. My point is everyone's personality is different. Now if you're a parent just watching, that's fine, but if you're a coach, now you need to get to know each child because you will be with them for a whole season, if not more. Knowing each child's personality goes a long way and can be helpful to a coach who is trying to get the most out of a child. For two years, I had a child in baseball and basketball who was a nervous wreck. He loved to play and always tried his best, but he always seemed to hold back for some reason. In baseball when he was pitching, I must have taken numerous trips out to the mound to talk to him and tell him just to pitch and not worry about anything else. I'd tell him to have fun, and no matter what, win or lose, he still had to go to school the next day, and that was the important part: Playing baseball is fun, so enjoy it. Now when you consider you're only allowed one trip out per inning because if you go out there a second time, you have to take the pitcher out, so I'll let you think about how much of my talking to him was done from the dugout. It all worked itself out. Even though it was not the goal when we started the season, he ended up pitching us to the championship. In case you're wondering, the number one goal at the grammar school level is to develop the player so that he has fun, learn, and prepares for high school. Winning is secondary.

Now let's look at the personality from a coach's point of view. If this same kid was coached by a person who put winning ahead of everything else, do you think the results would have been the same? If this coach was hard on this kid and yelled at him constantly instead of talking him through it, I doubt he would have achieved the same results. At the time, this boy was ten or eleven. It's a known fact that 80 percent of children playing sports quit by time they are twelve. One of the main reasons is pressure — pressure from their coaches, their parents, or their friends.

The personality of the parent also comes into play. The parent should be concerned of her child's well-being and that she is doing well in school. Sports to a parent should be fun for her child, not an ultimatum. What I mean by that is, you might have a parent who did very well in sports as a child but fell just short of making her high school, college, or even a professional career. So now she tries to live out her dream through her child. Then you have others who recognize their children are not good enough to play, so they discourage them. If the child wants to play, let her play as long as her grades are good. So what if she is not good? She is out there having fun, and as long as she is in the proper league, it's fun. In addition to playing, your child will learn how to interact with other children. He will learn what it means to be a part of a team by communicating with others on the team. That's what's important: watching your child grow through sports. It's not about winning. They learn what it likes to feel like to win, as well as the agony of defeat. Any coach that puts winning first at the grammar school level is not one you want for your child. Your child will only be a child for a short time that time goes by so quickly that you want him to enjoy it the very best he can. Putting pressure on the child to excel in sports is not what you or a coach should do. If your child gets a coach who puts pressure on him to do better or else he will not play, that is the time for you to step in and bring it to the attention of the league director or president. The goal at the grammar school level is to learn and improve; winning is secondary. In high school and college, it's entirely different, but at the grammar school level, it's always about the development of the child.

THE COACH'S CORNER

So you have a child interested in sports, and now it's time for you to sign her up with the local organization. After you checked out the organization and you feel comfortable with it, your child is ready to play sports that she enjoys with this organization. This is the grammar school level, so all coaches most likely are volunteers. These days they are doing it because their son or daughter is on the team and the organization needs coaches. Back when I played, all coaches were men and women who coached because they loved the game and wanted to make a difference in a child's life. They were former players of the organization or people who were a part of the parish who loved sports and wanted to coach. These days, with both parents working and trying to run the family, people just don't have the time they used to have, so organizations are forced to use anyone who wants to help. In some cases, it works out, but in other cases, it does not, and that's when the organization should step in, but it does not always happen. As I explain the meaning of the word coach and expand it, you will understand what I mean by the time I'm done with this chapter. If you look up the word coach in the dictionary, it has words like trainer, tutor, and instructor to define the word. All that is true, but a coach of a sports team is so much more than that. Coaching at any level has its similarities but yet is different. A coach is a motivator, but you would not motivate a ten-year-old the same way you would a sixteen-year-old. A coach is a disciplinarian, and the same thing goes here. The age you're coaching dictates how you discipline a child. For example you don't yell at an eight-year-old, but you might raise your voice to a fifteen-year-old. A coach is someone who teaches core values. Looking up the definition of coach, you don't see anything about core values. In addition to coaching the sport, they teach teamwork, sportsmanship, and more. Winning is always secondary at the young ages, and that's a main part of this book, so I want to stress that. Winning at the high school level has much more importance than winning at the grammar school level. At the grammar school level, you want the children to learn the sport and have fun. You want to teach them not only the sport but prepare them for when they go to high school. You put strong emphasis on core values, such as teamwork, sportsmanship, and more.

Now we are ready to break down what we spoke about even further. I spoke about the importance of having a good coach as opposed to having just someone whose kid is on the team so they offered to help. At the grammar school level, a good coach does not mean she is excellent at the sport and knows it inside and out. If you happen to get that, great, but if not, by good coach I mean someone who knows she is coaching young kids who are learning and wants to make sure they all get the most out of the season. A good coach not only teaches the sport but the core values. A good coach does not care what the score is; she cares about the progress of the team and all the kids on it. Now let's look at some examples from my forty years of coaching at the grammar school level. One time the basketball director asked me to take on an assistant. I was against it, but because the director was a good friend, I took him on. But I warned him it might not end well. The team was doing very well at the time of this incident; our record was 6-2. As a coach, I have many rules, and one of them is never beat a team badly, no matter who the opponent is, because you don't want to demoralize the kids on the other team. So if my team was ahead by ten or more points, I would take out the better players. Every time I did this, the opposing team would catch up, and this coach would come over to me and say, "Put the other kids back in." This went on for about a week until one night he came over. I resisted, and he came back and used the four-letter word. Right then and there I said, "Leave my bench and don't come back," and that's exactly what he did. Coach Bob McKillop of Davidson University in North Carolina once said he recruits interchangeable players. By that he means players who can play just about every position. This is exactly what coaches at the grammar school level are supposed to do. This is exactly what I was doing with this team, as well as all my teams I coached. Too many coaches focus on their so-called star player. What happens if that player can't make it? Will the team know what to do? Will they have confidence in each other, or will they be down on themselves because the so-called star is not there? This all depends on who the coach of the team is. If the coach is a motivator and preaches teamwork, discipline, and all the core values, they can play well enough to compete. They may not win, but it's not about winning at this level, it's about teaching. The next example I can give you is from a close friend of mine who coached his son's team from third to eighth grades. This team had one player who was a cut above the rest, but because the coach did not emphasize the core values enough, this kid got away with everything. So now the kid goes to high school and gets cut from the team at the very first tryout the very first day by the high school coach because of his mouth. The coach told them to do something, he made a wisecrack remark, and out the door he went. I blame this on the grammar school coach, and I still rib him about it today. Teaching the core values we speak about here are so important, but some grammar school coaches only look at the wins and losses and that's it. This kid who had a chance with a high school team now has nothing and could end up in the street and get in trouble, and I blame the grammar school coach.

In another example, the director did not have a coach for one of the in-house eighth grade teams, so he took one of the board members who did not volunteer but just accepted it because his son was on the team. The team did not learn anything. The coach just leaned up against the wall and said nothing. All he did was make the substitutions. He never instructed the players on what they were doing wrong. He never gave them a plan; he just let each game go and waited for the season to end. The director and president just let it go without doing anything. This is the type of coach you want to avoid. Remember, you want your child to learn and have fun, but you're paying money for him to enjoy himself, and you have every right to approach the league director or president in this case and get this situation changed.

There are times the parents need to stay in the background, and we will talk about that at some point, but in cases like this, you should bring it to the director's attention.

Every team I coach gets the exact same speech with their parents there at the very first official practice. I tell them they are there to have fun, they are there to learn, and we are going to win and lose games. The grammar school level is about teaching, learning, and having fun. If we happen to win, it's an added bonus because no matter win or lose, the next day they have to get up and go to school, and that's what counts most.

CORE VALUES

This book talks about sports starting from the young age of five and going through the high school years. However, its main focus is the grammar school years. No matter what sport your child is playing, in addition to the sport, it is extremely important that the coaches stress core values just as much and from the very beginning.

Only in this chapter I am not only going to talk about core values for the children but for the coaches and parents as well. In my opinion, for the most part in today's sports, core values are a lost art. I say this because coaches forget why they are there, and they put winning ahead of everything else. When coaching a sport, it's not only about that sport but more importantly about teaching the children how to act and how not to act. So I will now go through core values, starting with the children and ending with the parents — with the coaches in between both of them.

When talking about core values, I have so many to pick from, but I narrowed it down to four for the children. My top four are teamwork, sportsmanship, commitment, and appreciation.

No matter what sport I was coaching, one of my most famous lines to the kids throughout the season was, "There is no I in 'team'." During the season, I would ask different kids to spell the word team. Then I asked them what letter was not in there that I was looking for, and without hesitation they not only would say "I," but they would repeat my line of, "There is no I in 'team'."

It's important for a coach to get the message of teamwork into his or her players from the very start. The quicker the players get it, the better. If you have one or two who don't get it, then you have to spend time getting that across to them, and it takes away from the overall progress of the team.

For example one child might be much better than the rest, so he thinks he can do what he wants. As a coach, you have to put a stop to it or you risk losing the other players. They see one get away with something, and they want to do the same.

So you first explain it to the child that he or she has to be a team player. If that does not work, then you have to do things that I don't like to do, but when necessary, you have to punish the child to some degree.

One way is with less playing time than everyone else. Then the last resort is sitting the child down with the parent, and I can say I never had to go that far in my thirty-plus years of coaching. I hope it never gets to this point, but you want all the kids to understand it's not about one player but about every player on the team. We win and lose as a team, and we learn as the season goes along.

Next up is sportsmanship. You need the kids to understand they have to respect their opponents. Some youth organizations have a bad name because of the way they act while playing a game, no matter what the sport is.

Let your kids know they are not only representing themselves but the name on their uniforms. Get them to understand when other organizations hear your name, they want them to say they do it right and they are a pleasure to play against.

You teach the kids to be humble in victory and gracious in defeat. You don't want them to show off or be sore losers. Teach your kids to shake hands with the opposing team before and after the game. Teach them to help an opposing player up if he or she falls during the game.

The next one for the children is commitment. No matter what the sport they decide to try, they must be committed to it for the whole season.

They can't say after two weeks they don't like it and quit. Of course they can, but by letting the child do this, you're saying it's fine to quit. That's the wrong message because then they think they can do that with other things as well.

YOUR GUIDE IN YOUTH SPORTS

Explain to them that the league has to make the teams, and when you're part of a team, you're committed to that team for the whole season. It's important not only to make the games but the practices as well. This is why it's important that when you're starting out, you and the child have a good feel for the sport you will try. Explain to them the coaches and director's work hard for them to play and have fun, so it's important for her to be committed to the team.

The last core value I selected for the children is appreciation. They must learn all that is involved in getting them to and from practices — all the sacrifices you as parents and the coaches make to get to the games and practices.

If they want to skip a practice or a game to be with another group of friends, this is unacceptable. It's important that they learn all the effort the grown-ups are putting in so they can have fun and play a team sport.

Not only your time, but also explain that it costs money too for them to play. They might be young, but teaching them these values at a young age will go a long way as they get older.

The four core values I came up with for coaches are as follows: responsibility, passion, unity, and commitment.

No matter what sport you're coaching, you are responsible for all the children in terms of safety, surroundings, and more. If you're in a gym, you should make sure the floor is not wet. Make sure there are no loose objects on the floor. If you're on a baseball field or any field outdoors, the same rules apply. You look for loose objects and holes in the outfield. Coaching does not mean just taking the team for an hour or two and that's it. Many other things come into play. For instance once practice or a game is over, are all your kids accounted for with a ride home? If not you are the one responsible. You can't leave until everyone is accounted for. You're also responsible for how you act on and off the playing field. As we speak of in other areas in the book, a team will take on the personality of its coach. If you curse or hound officials, the children will do the same and you don't want that. You want them to learn and have fun.

The next one for coaches is passion. As a coach, you have to want to be there. You can't say yes, I will coach just because your child is on the team or just because that will put you on the playing field with your child. Also as a coach, you have to coach all the kids equally, not just your child. Being a youth coach means you're willing to give up your time and make sacrifices. It's not just one or two hours a week and that's it.

You have to want to be there. You have to want to teach these kids. If you just go there and go through the motions, the kids and parents will sense that, and then bigger issues will arise. Kids will complain they are not learning; parents will complain they are wasting their money.

Don't just agree to coach just to coach because coaching is not for everyone.

Next up for coaches is unity. Whatever sport you're coaching, you want that team to come together as one. The closer your team is, the better it is for you and everyone on the team. They will learn faster and have fun doing it. In some cases, you will be together for four or five years. You want that togetherness. Once you have a set routine, the team will know it by heart, and it will become easier for everyone involved.

For example practice on the same nights and at the same time the whole season. Have a system for playing time. Have a set of rules for the team to follow.

Last up is commitment. It's a repeat one you saw listed for the kids. Well if the kids have to be committed, so do the coaches. A coach can't say, "I don't want to practice today. I want to stay home and rest." By doing this, you're setting a bad example, and kids will start to do the same by skipping practices.

I can't tell you how many trips with friends I missed because of my commitment to the kids. If I'm the coach, I am expected to be there. Don't accept to coach and then put everything on your assistant coach. That is poor judgement. Think before you accept to coach a team, and that goes for any level.

The last group of core values are for the parents. Now you would think that you should not have any issues with the parents at all. That is so far from the truth, it's incredible, especially in this day and age.

When I played, it was rare a parent got involved and interfered with the coach. There was no violence or fights in the stands that we hear about today. No one ever threated a coach back in the day; these things were just unheard of.

I came up with three words to use as core values for parents. The first one is honesty. I want to use honesty with a double meaning. First the parents should be honest with the organization and the coach because they need to know any important information pertaining to the child. For example are there any kind of health issues they need to be aware of?

I can't tell you how many kids I had with some kind of issue and the parents never acknowledged it. By not saying anything, the parents are not doing right by all involved. They could be putting other children in danger by not saying anything. It's not fair to the organization, the coaches, or the children on their child's team.

Then there can also be situations where the parents are not being honest with themselves. All children deserve to play, but not all children are of equal talent.

A parent needs to understand where their child belongs when it comes to placing them on a team. For example if you have an A and a B team, it is no shame to play on the B team where the children are less talented than those on the A team.

I can't tell you how many parents refuse to see the light. In some cases, because of the stubbornness of the parents, it's hard to form the B team. One time I had to work so hard for one parent to see that her son belonged on the B team that if it was not for the director, it might not have happened.

All parents need to remember when they sign their children up for youth sports, it's about the children. All parties involved should always have the best interest of the children.

Unfortunately today some people forget that. You have parents who see something in their child that is not there. You have coaches who forget about core values and put winning first.

Youth sports is about developing the child, not only in that particular sport but preparing them for life lessons as well.

The second one for the parents is respect. Too many parents today get too involved instead of just being spectators. If they think they can do better, then sign up to coach at registration. Organizations are always looking for coaches. The problem is they don't want to put in all the time, effort, and energy its takes to coach, but they want to criticize the coach or, worse yet, verbally or physically abuse them.

In this day and age, there have been many documented cases of parents abusing coaches. It is a total disgrace and should not be tolerated at any level. There are even cases where there are fights in the stands among the fans. Really? This is youth sports; it should be about the kids, not about the winning and losing.

Last up for the parents is dependability. These are young kids; they can't get to the practices and games unless accompanied by an adult.

So if you sign your child up, it's up to you to make sure he gets to his practices and games on time. On time does not mean when it starts — it means when the coach says to get there.

If you can't get your child there, make arrangements with a relative a neighbor or another parent who has a child on the team.

Some parents have a lot to say, yet they show up late, don't show up at all, and don't even have the decency to contact the coach to let them know.

THE DIFFERENT LEVELS OF PLAY

There are many different levels in youth sports, and we will take a closer look at each one.

First there is instructional. This is an introduction to whatever sport your child is playing. In baseball they might call it tee ball, where the coach puts the ball on a tee and your child takes a swing at the ball while the ball is set in one place. They do this so it's easier for the child to hit the ball as opposed to someone throwing the ball for them to hit. They also use rubber baseballs so the child does not get hurt.

In basketball they use adjustable rims for the kids to shoot at and use smaller basketballs.

The point is, at this level where the child is four or five years old, you want to make it as fun as possible so that they come back. You don't want to push them; you want to give them encouragement and confidence.

The coach should create a relaxed environment here and give a few two-minute breaks during the session. Remember, at this age, the child attention span is short, and you need to mix things up and keep them interested.

Next you have in-house leagues. This is when the organization you signed your child up with splits up the kids by age groups and forms teams to compete against each other. Some organizations do two-year age groups, some do three. I prefer two-year age groups because sometimes a three-year gap can be too much in terms of competitiveness. I don't expect a ten-year-old to go up against a thirteen-year-old.

To have a well-run in-house league, all teams should be balanced. If after four games, one team is 0-4 and another is 4-0, a change should be made. I can't tell you how many times directors just let the season go. The final standing would have one team 14-0 while another team ended up 2-12. Did the 2-12 team have fun, and what did the 14-0 team learn? It thinks it is invincible. This is not what you want. It's your own league; you want balance throughout from top to bottom. It's important to remember that in in-house leagues, you are teaching core values: teamwork, sportsmanship, commitment, and more. It's not fun if a child is going home all the time with her head down because her team lost again.

Now we get to travel teams, and this is where its gets difficult if the team is not handled right. The definition of a travel team is one that plays other schools from your area and even other parts of the city. Travel teams normally take the best kids from your organization at each age level. Basketball is strictly one-year, but baseball is a two-year age limit.

Most organizations hold tryouts for these teams; some organizations get just enough to have a team. The most important thing for a parent if your child makes the team is to feel out the coach from the very start. Some take ten kids or more on a basketball team while only five can play at a time. Now if your child is really good, he will play, so you don't have an issue, but what if your child is borderline and the coach takes ten kids. How much is your child going to play? This is why you have to be there and listen to how the coach runs his team. If you're paying money and your child is showing up and not playing much, maybe travel ball is a mistake.

Nine is the best number in terms of basketball, but you can go with ten — anything over ten, if you intend to play each child, is tough. I tell my parents right from the start *all* my kids play, and I try to do it equally even if it is travel. Most coaches do not do that because it's all about winning for them. This is travel, and it is more competitive, but all kids should play, at least by my standards.

Baseball has more spots to fill, but still sometimes a coach takes fifteen kids on a travel team and the back end of the roster sees limited playing time. Those kids who don't play get discouraged, and some end up quitting. This is why whatever the sport, if your child is playing travel, make sure they belong because if they don't, there is no shame in just playing in-house.

The next group to discuss is the AAU travel teams. Unlike the coaches of your local organizations, these coaches are getting paid to coach. If your child wants to play here, I suggest you take a hard look before you sign them up. Coaches here are not obligated in any way to play all the kids. They coach to win at all costs while teaching the game. If your child is exceptional and has sights on playing high school ball, she belongs here, but she has to understand the commitment she is making. You're playing the best of the best at your age bracket — there is no slacking off any time for anything else. It's schoolwork and this team; it involves a lot of travelling, sometimes out of state, so your child has to be dedicated. Otherwise if not, you're wasting time and, more importantly, money — your hard-earned money. If your child is serious and dedicated and really wants to play in high school, you should look into a local AAU team. You can also let them work out with a local coach over the summer; it will most likely be cheaper and far less travelling for everyone. The best thing to do is sit down and figure out first if your child is really committed and then decide which path to take.

The final level to talk about is high school. The few years I coached at this level, I was very surprised. I was coaching girls' junior varsity basketball at a high school that played level-two competitions. We were in the gym five or six days a week from November through February and sometimes March, depending how far we went into the playoffs. It's very competitive no matter what level your high school team is playing at. Unlike grammar school, a coach does not have to play everyone. If you make your high school team, that right there is an accomplishment. If you want to play, you have to earn it. If you go to practice, give it your all, and don't get in much, and this bothers you, then you have three choices. One, you can discuss it with the coach, but you better have your facts straight. Two, you can keep working at it and support your team, or you can quit and focus more on your studies. I go with option two here because it's a sport you played all your life, and it's an honor to make your high school team. However, if you feel you're busting your butt and missing time with friends, it's totally your call here. As a parent, in this case just be supportive of your child's decision, especially if the school marks are good.

LET'S TALK NUMBERS

Throughout the book, you hear me saying the same things whenever I feel it's appropriate.

You hear me saying it's about the kids — all the kids. You hear me saying it's about learning and having fun, not winning.

I say don't live out your dream through your child. Let him create his own legacy. I say as long as he is doing well in school, that's what matters most.

I speak about core values and lessons that the children can take with them well beyond their playing days.

All these parents who get personal training for their children, are they doing it for themselves or the children? Why does a nine-year-old need a personal trainer? Let her have a normal childhood. Letting a child play one sport all year round is the wrong thing to do. You might burn the child out.

History shows that when starting a child in sports at four or five, that same child is turned off by twelve or thirteen years old. Let's look at some numbers to support all that I have been saying.

The number of parents who hope their children play high school sports is 26 percent. In families with incomes of less than fifty thousand dollars, that same number spikes up to 39 percent. These parents, as well as all parents, should focus more on their children's' education than if they play high school sports.

It's great if the child does play, but if not, so be it — focus on education. Take a look at the following numbers, and you will understand why I say that.

Only one out of 168 high school players get drafted in baseball.

Only one out of 2,451 boys who played high school basketball gets drafted by the NBA.

Only 1.6 percent of college football seniors get drafted by the NFL. As for high school seniors, the number of those getting drafted is 0.08 percent.

So just by looking at those numbers, I ask one question: Why go to great lengths and make your child do things he doesn't want to do?

If he wants to, fine, but most of the time it's the parents making the call.

I say let your child be a child. Don't take her childhood away from her with a rigorous sports routine.

If she plays high school sports, great — if not, so be it. The education is what is important, not what sport you want her to play.

POLITICS IN YOUTH SPORTS

I'm disappointed that I even have to spend time on this topic, but unfortunately politics in youth sports exists.

Let's start from the very beginning, going back to when we spoke about the different levels of play. In that portion of the book, we spoke about the organizations' in-house leagues.

If you remember, I said an in-house league is all the kids in a certain age group from the organization you joined who compete against each other. In the end, the winners will get a jacket, a sweatshirt, or a trophy, depending on what the organization decides.

Now as parents of your first child, this is all new to you. You would think the directors would make the teams fair, and if after a few games adjustments need to be made, they make them. By adjustments I mean taking a child from a team that was let's say 4-0 and moving that child to a team that was 0-4.

The reason this should be done is to balance the league; it's not about winning.

Yet we get directors that stack their own teams and shortchange another team. They do this for a few reasons. One, trying to please the parents who travel together. This way the boys are on the same team and the schedules match. So what if it makes one team too strong? They overlook that to keep certain parents and coaches happy.

Another scenario might be one child has a friend who wants to play, but he has to play with that child. That's fine if it does not make the team too strong or weak. If it does, the director should say it can't happen, but most of the time, they say nothing. Now it's fine for that team, but what about the other teams in the league? Is it fair to them?

When I look at an in-house league standings in any sport, no team should be undefeated, and no team should be winless. It's your league; you control it. In the world of travel ball, it's anything goes. That should not be the case here. I will say in some cases it might happen even with balanced teams, but if done right, that is very rare.

Another reason it might happen is because it's a director's kid who is in question. Her dad wants her on a certain team, and since the dad is a director, it's allowed to happen. Totally unacceptable in my opinion — just another thing you might see along the way.

Then when we get to high school, it might be even worse. When a child or grandchild had a dad or grandfather who is an alumni of the school and donates a large sum of money to the school, I've seen exceptions made for that child.

If the child deserves a spot on the team, that's fine, but in some cases, the child clearly does not belong there. What is overlooked is the kid who lost out on the last spot who was clearly better than the kid who made the team for the wrong reason.

So now you get the idea of why I spent time talking about politics in youth sports. In my opinion, it should not exist. If you feel it does where you're at, you are free to leave — just wait for the season to end. Then the following year look for another organization.

CONVERSATIONS AND QUOTES ALONG THE WAY

It took me three years to put this guide together, mostly because I stopped in 2017. I guess you can say I got lazy or I had a serious case of writer's block.

Anyway, during the three years, I ran into people who gave me ideas or supported the reason why this guide needed to be done. These are in no specific order, so here we go.

There was an executive of a company whom I met in the elevator going home on a Friday night. We talked about what we had planned for the weekend, and he said he had to coach his twelve-year-old twin girls in basketball.

He followed that up with, "My wife says I get too emotional. I need to calm down on the sidelines." My reply was, "She's right. It's not about winning; it's about the kids." So from that two-minute conversation came coach's corner.

I also met a brother of one of my former players, and he asked me where I was coaching these days. I asked why, and he said because he was thinking about signing up his son. My first question was, how old is your son, and he said three.

Let me tell you, I went off on him in a nice way. By now if you read the guide, you know what I mean. I told him, "You play with him. Why would you want to sign him up so young?" I brought up the child's attention span and the money factor. He walked away with something to think about, I will say that much.

Then I was talking to a parent of one of the boys on my current team. He talks about this video he saw and from that came coach's kid.

The next story took place while I was on vacation with a bunch of former players and their kids. We were at dinner, and the coaches were talking about the team.

One coach said, "My one goal for this winter is to get this one kid to come play for us next year." What he saying is he wants to recruit a kid from an opposing team in the travel league they play in.

1 did not say a word. I just sat there in amazement because this guy was an educator in a high school, and here he was talking about recruiting a ten-year-old kid.

My thought was, what about the kids you have on the team now? Focus on those kids. Make them better; don't try and get better kids because you will be pushing some young kid to the background.

Now if a kid was moving away or was not coming back, then you get this kid. However, the combination of this coach and talking about recruiting just left me in shock.

See, this wasn't just another youth coach. This guy is, in my opinion, one of the top two youth coaches I know. For example if coaching a team was a whole pizza pie, he cuts it into fifty slices while coaches like me cut it into ten slices. His knowledge, combined with the way he handles the kids, is a cut above most youth coaches I know. Yet he talking about recruiting a ten-year-old.

Then there was another vacation trip, and we have another father-coach talking about upgrading his son's upcoming nine-year-old team.

His son's eight-year-old basketball team, which had thirteen kids on it, just finished its season going 4-2 in a double-elimination tournament. The team played all its games during the season without keeping score because it was league rules. However, every parent knew the score.

So the season-ending tournament, which kept score, was to prepare them for the following year.

So September rolls around, and he adds five kids, and now that team has eighteen kids. You can only play five kids at a time. End result was they got three more kids and made two teams, but it was the wrong thing to do. Then the following year, he decides his son wants to focus on baseball, and the directors are left to figure it out.

Then there was the coworker who said to me one day she just had gotten her twenty-one-month-old an iPad. You know I went off on her too in a nice way.

It just blows me away how today parents just think giving kids a computerized item solves everything.

Then there was the situation that sparked the idea for this book. The president of an organization refused to sit and meet with the coaches because he wanted nothing to do with the sport in question.

Of course the coaches stayed. If it were me, I'd be long gone. How sad when grown-ups can't sit down and come to terms to benefit the children — all the children.

VIOLENCE IN YOUTH SPORTS

Just like I did not like talking about politics in youth sports, I don't enjoy this topic either. However, the truth is it exists and can't be ignored.

Why does it exist? There could be a number of reasons. A parent is not happy with his child's playing time on the team. Or parents of opposing teams can get into a heated argument that turns into a brawl.

No matter what the case may be, it should not exist, but it does because parents forget what youth sports is supposed to be about.

Some think their children will go on to get a college scholarship after high school. In terms of numbers, fewer than 1 percent of all high school seniors go on to get full scholarships to college.

Notice all my examples involve parents; the kids are really not the problem. It's the parents who think they know more than the coaches or the officiating crew, and they cause problems.

Here are some examples. This one I witnessed with my own eyes when I was fourteen years old. My cousin's baseball team was in Forest Park, Georgia, playing in the World Series for thirteen-year-olds. They are playing the host team in an elimination game. It was a tie game, but every close call just seemed to go to the host team.

There was a close play at home plate, and the runner was called out. The third base coach, after saying a few choice words to the home plate umpire, charged down the third base line and cracked him one.

This not only ended the game but caused a riot in the stands and on the field. There is no place for this stuff, but again it's a case of grown-ups putting winning ahead of the children.

I could understand saying something to the official but keep it short and professional. As a coach, I learned one thing when challenging officials in any sport: You have a better chance of challenging a rule than a call.

Professionals coaches will say winning isn't everything — it's the only thing. That might be true in professional sports but not in youth sports.

Youth sports should be about many things — winning is the least among them. By reading this guide, you know I speak core values and building a child's confidence before speaking about winning at this level.

Some of the stories I hear about are insane. A coach attacking a referee at a big youth championship football game. The kids are five and six years old; they can't even run plays, but yet it's a big championship game.

A father who took a gun onto the football field in Pennsylvania. Another father in California who ran onto the field and knocked a kid over.

This all happens because parents lose perspective of what youth sports is all about.

THE SURVEY SAYS

I came up with the idea to ask the following questions to a random group of people involved in youth sports. My thinking was all these people had heard me talk about doing this book, so I figured, why not get them involved?

So I came up with three questions, the first one being a three-part question.

How would you describe the state of youth sports today as compared to when you grew up? What's better? What's worse?

Should sports be a part of every child's life? Why?

What would you say to parents who say they don't want their kids playing sports? They want them doing something that will benefit them when they get older.

So I took the answers from those who responded and put them right here.

Most all responders said parents today are a big problem. Some talk about technology being a problem.

As for what's good, some said more options for kids today. We understand more today than we did years ago about the human body, which is a plus today in sports.

Some talked about the different times and the generation gaps, which are a reason for the way things are today.

Well you take a look, and I hope you enjoy the various responses to the questions.

JOHN A. DEANGELO

Youth sports to me has two definitions. One is organized, and the other is kids just having pickup games. What I like about youth sports today is there are so many different options to play in youth sports. When I was younger, there were no lacrosse or flag football leagues. And there were few soccer leagues. I believe each township does it best to get kids involved in youth sports to keep the kids active and also try to keep the kids out of trouble.

I do not see many kids playing outside these days and have pickup games. I believe there are several reasons. First, obviously the video games and phones have taken over these kids' lives. If you walk down the street, check and see how many kids are looking at their phone.

Second, like I said before, there are so many different options of sports/leagues you can play today. I know several kids who play three to four different sports, then have to go home and do homework. There is no time to go outside and play with their friends in pickup games.

The thing I do not like about youth sports today is the parents. They are too serious. Every game to them is the World Series or the Super Bowl. They fight, scream at the officials, other parents, and even little kids who are playing the game. As a parent, you should be a role model, but acting this way is just ridiculous.

Growing up I remember playing one organized sport and had a blast. I remember being outside with my friends just about every day, and we played sports all the time. We never played cops and robbers or cowboys and Indians; it was always sports. As we got older, we stayed friends, and even though we became adults, we joined an organized sports program.

When I was younger, I never remember the parents ever getting out of hand. I do remember the parents cheering, but I never saw them yell at another parent or a kid. Yes when there was a controversial call, the parents did speak their minds.

I do believe sports should be part of every child's life, first and foremost for health reasons. Also it teaches them to be part of a team. When a child gets older and goes into the real world, most jobs involve being a part of a team. This is a good way to introduce the child before he gets older. Also from my experience of coaching, I see leaders come from being a part of a team. This will also help them as they get older.

Also I believe even though sports are fun, it can be hard to reach their goal, whatever that may be (scoring a touchdown, hitting a home run, or winning a championship). If you don't succeed at first, you keep fighting to reach your goal. Don't ever quit.

Friendships and memories are also made from being a part of a team, which til this day I still have both.

I would tell a parent to please think about having his or her kid play a sport. As I mentioned before, it is a good learning experience being a part of a team.

Our generation gets credit for killing youth sports by getting too involved. The lessons learned have little to do with the sport, but more importantly we learned how to be a good teammate, how to be resilient, and how losing actually helped us.

Kids haven't changed — but parents should stay away.

Should sports be a part of every child life? Why?
Not necessarily — there are many other ways to learn valuable lessons.

What would you say to parents who say they don't want their kids playing sports, they want them doing something that will benefit them as they get older?
They should encourage their kid to try everything and make sure he or she is active, hanging with good kids, and being mature.

I find that the state of youth sports today, as opposed to when I was growing up, is in a rapid decline. This comes from too many kids being involved in video games instead of playing sports. When I grew up, we were outdoors; today kids stay in and play video games.

We played games kids today never even heard of: stickball, dodge ball, stoop ball, whiffle ball, and more.

All children should play sports in some capacity. Team sports is important because they learn how to work with other children, and it keeps them off the computer. It's a good way to get exercise as opposed to sitting at home playing video games.

The parents today are another big issue that you did not see when I was a kid. Today they are too intense; it puts too much pressure on the child. The kids are supposed to have fun.

How would you describe the state of youth sports today as compared to when you grew up?

In a word, challenged. The biggest difference is the explosion and domination of technology in a child's life. To get them to pick up a baseball bat or a basketball, you first have to get them to put down their iPhone or iPad, which is not the easiest of tasks. Plus, where youth sports used to be an important early vehicle for a child to meet new friends and learn socialization skills, that too is being usurped by technology, specifically the social media platforms. Look at how technology has even redefined the word "sport" itself with the popularity and mainstream acceptance of e-sports and gaming.

What's better? What worse?
No doubt the growth and deserved respect given to girls' youth athletics is so much better today than in generations past. On the flip side, I think what is worse, especially in the cities of the Northeast and Midwest, is the collateral damage done by the decline in Catholic parochial schools. This has had a trickle-down effect on youth sports leagues since the church, for many generations, was a key supporter of youth sports organizations in major metropolitan areas.

Should sports be a part of every child's life? Why?
Sports should be introduced and available to every child but never forced. Obviously it won't be for everyone, but every child should get to have an initial, and hopefully positive, experience with organized sports and then make up his or her own mind if he or she likes it and wants to continue further. The key is to make sure the opportunities exist for those who desire it.

What would you say to parents who say they don't want their kids playing sports, they want them doing something that will benefit them as they get older?
I would respectfully tell them that the thesis of their question is off base and illogical. Sportsmanship, teamwork, structure, and healthy competition are just a few of the skills a child will learn in organized sports that I have no doubt will be beneficial skills that will last a lifetime. Also I would remind them of the universal health benefits of an active childhood through sports.

I think that parents today want immediate satisfaction, and because of that fact, they just want their kids to show up and win and come to practice or games when it is convenient for them.

YOUR GUIDE IN YOUTH SPORTS

I think sports is very important for kids, and they should play as many sports as possible to see what they are interested in and learn teamwork and how to lose as well as win with respect. Today I feel there is more money being made in youth sports, and playing can become very expensive. There are fewer and fewer in-house leagues, and more time and money is focused on travel and tournaments, which hurts some kids who want to learn and have fun.

The key is to find good organizations with good coaches who want to teach, love the game, and have a genuine interest in the kids to get better and grow as athletes and be respectful adults someday. Daddy ball is tough to navigate and is frustrating, especially if the dad who is coaching is delusional and has his own agenda that does not include the interest of the team or the kids around him.

Having three kids who enjoy playing sports, I do not have the answers yet, but the wife and I do our best to get the kids to different organizations to surround them with people who can help them grow as respectful men and good athletes.

How would you describe the state of youth sports today as compared to when you grew up?

In some ways better and in some ways worse. Parents are more involved today than in years past, which can be good or bad depending on the attitude of the parent. Moms seem to be much more involved than in earlier years. The kids are also involved in way more activities now than in earlier years, which causes them more stress and makes it harder on coaches. More parents seem to be under the impression today that youth sports will lead to scholarships.

Should sports be a part of every child's life? Why?

If a child is interested in sports, it should be a part of his/her life. It helps to develop a sense of discipline, teamwork, and camaraderie. It also provides exercise and an escape of screens and monitors.

What would you say to parents who say they don't want their kids playing sports, they want them doing something that will benefit them as they get older?

I would tell parents that they should play for the reasons described above. And these reasons will benefit them as they get older. If parents volunteer to coach, they will also get the added benefit of parent-child bonding.

How would you describe the state of youth sports today as compared to when you grew up?

When I grew up, the level of parental involvement was much less significant. I felt that a lot of "practices" were really just time for fun in an organized environment. A portion of the practices would start with some skill drills, but there was always plenty of practice time to simply play and enjoy the sport.

Today community sports organizations are highly organized, and many more parents are involved. The prime emphasis at practices is to hone your skills for a specific position, one which, it seems, you're destined to play until the end of time. Kids specialize at an earlier and earlier age.

What's better? What worse?

I think there are advantages to more parents/coaches being involved, and it can help the kids develop faster with more guidance and bring them closer to older people in their community who truly care about kids.

Many practices and teams are no longer fun but work. That is why many eleven-year-olds are already "burned out" from a sport, and many may never play it again.

Should sports be a part of every child's life? Why?

I believe sports should be a part of every child's life — or at least they should be given the opportunity. If there's no real interest or desire, it should not be forced upon them. But in most cases, I believe sports help to gain strength, coordination, and great friendships. Sports early in life can set a healthy example/path for the rest of one's life.

What would you say to parents who say they don't want their kids playing sports, they want them doing something that will benefit them as they get older?

I'm in my mid-fifties, and sports remain one of the greatest joys and benefits in my life. I believe sports add to a truly full, rich life. Work and many other aspects of life can be very stressful. Playing sports is one of the greatest stress relievers I know. From both the physical and mental perspectives, there's nothing better than sports for me.

FINAL THOUGHTS

As I stated in the beginning and in the title, this is just a guide for parents with young children starting out in sports.

This guide was put together through my forty years of being involved in youth sports. I am not a professional coach or expert; I am a youth coach. I took stories and experiences and included them in here where I saw fit.

Although I discuss the high school level and the various upscale leagues, this guide is primarily for children in grammar school. It's also for the parents of these children to use as a guide — what to look for and what to do in certain situations. The purpose of youth sports is to learn and have fun, not be in any way a burden on the child or the parents.

I hope you enjoyed reading this as much as I enjoyed putting it together. I hope this helps all parents to some degree as they get their children involved in youth sports. If you took one thing from this book and it helped, then my mission was a success.

I'm sure there are some coaches and directors out there who will read this and say, "This guy is old. It's not done that way anymore." Truth is, with young children it should always be about teaching, learning, and having fun, not winning at all costs. It should be about implementing core values at a young age so that they take these life lessons with them and use them as they get older.